W9-BFZ-748

PASSPORT
JAPAN

Passport to the World

Passport Argentina
Passport Brazil
Passport China
Passport France
Passport Germany
Passport Hong Kong
Passport India
Passport Indonesia
Passport Israel
Passport Italy
Passport Korea
Passport Mexico
Passport Philippines
Passport Poland
Passport Russia
Passport Singapore
Passport South Africa
Passport Spain
Passport Taiwan
Passport Thailand
Passport United Kingdom
Passport USA
Passport Vietnam

PASSPORT
JAPAN

Your Pocket Guide
to
**Japanese Business,
Customs & Etiquette**

**Dean Engel
Ken Murakami
Contributing Editor: Patrick Bray**

Passport Series Editor: Barbara Szerlip

WORLD TRADE PRESS®
Professional Books for International Trade

World Trade Press
1450 Grant Avenue, Suite 204
Novato, California 94945 USA
Tel: (415) 898-1124
Fax: (415) 898-1080
USA Order Line: (800) 833-8586
E-mail: worldpress@aol.com
http://www.worldtradepress.com
http://www.globalroadwarrior.com

"Passport to the World" concept: Edward Hinkelman
Cover design: Peter Jones
Illustrations: Tom Watson

This publication is designed to provide general information concerning the cultural aspects of doing business with people from a particular country. It is sold with the understanding that the publisher is not engaged in rendering legal or any other professional services. If legal advice or other expert assistance is required, the services of a competent professional person should be sought.

Library of Congress Cataloging-in-Publication Data
Engel, Dean
Passport Japan: Your Pocket Guide to Business, Customs & Etiquette/ Dean Engel, Ken Murakami.
p. cm.
ISBN 1-885073-17-8
1.Corporate culture --Japan. 2.Business etiquette -- Japan.
3. Industrial management -- Social aspects -- Japan.
4. Negotiation in business -- Japan. 5. Intercultural communication. I. Murakami, Ken 1934- . II. Title.
HD58.7.E445 1996
395'.52 -- dc20
96-360
CIP

Printed in the United States of America

Table of Contents
Japan
Land of the Rising Sun

 Doing Business Across Cultures

Internationally Speaking

The past decade has seen a dramatic lowering of trade barriers, the globalization of markets and explosive growth in international trade. The business world has become increasingly interdependent, creating both new challenges and exciting new opportunities.

In order to conduct business abroad, you need to understand the environments in which your foreign counterparts operate. You will probably never know a particular culture as well as your own — not only is the language different, but the historical and cultural context within which its people operate is often misunderstood by outsiders.

But even a little bit of knowledge can help you develop closer, more successful relationships with your associates. And your international transactions will be far more enjoyable as a result.

Think Globally, Act Locally

Although business operations have become highly internationalized, national and local traditions, attitudes and beliefs remain diverse. Everyone's perceptions — what we see, hear, taste, touch and smell — are filtered through a particular set of beliefs and assumptions.

When you understand that your own cultural background colors your world view, you can begin to appreciate that your foreign associate may have an entirely different perspective, and that he or she may approach a situation in a totally different and unexpected way.

For example, whereas Westerners tend to value individuality of thought and action, Eastern cultures prize conformity and harmony of purpose. While an Englishman's primary focus may be to conclude the business at hand, a Hong Kong Chinese will concentrate on first developing a personal relationship. Public praise is much enjoyed by North Americans, but it is a source of embarrassment and discomfort for Japanese. Failure to recognize these inherent differences will result in misconceptions and inappropriate responses that can doom a business relationship.

The Cross-Cultural Key

Cross-cultural understanding will allow you to recognize important hints and undercurrents that can have a profound effect on the outcome of your transactions. For example, silence at a negotiating table can signify a number of different things. In Japan, silence might mean that your counterparts are seriously considering what has just been said, or it might be a bargaining ploy. In the U.S., it usually signals a great deal of discomfort and unhappiness about the way things are going.

Gaining a thorough understanding of a people can take several years of living and working among them — and sometimes not even that is sufficient.

Comparing Values Across Cultures

One Culture:	Another Culture:
Values change	Values tradition
Favors specific communication	Favors ambiguous communication
Values analytical, linear problem solving	Values intuitive, lateral problem solving
Places emphasis on individual performance	Places emphasis on group performance
Considers verbal communication most important	Considers context & nonverbal communication most important
Focuses on task and product	Focuses on relationship and process
Places emphasis on promoting differing views	Places emphasis on harmony and consensus
Emphasizes competition	Emphasizes collaboration
Prefers informal tone	Prefers formal tone
Is flexible about schedules	Emphasizes rigid adherence to schedule

However, you can increase your chances of achieving harmonious and profitable relationships by learning something about your associate's point of view and adjusting your behavior accordingly.

Getting Along

Anyone who has traveled to another country has probably experienced an embarrassing moment or two caused by a cultural misconception or misunderstanding. To some extent, these are unavoidable and can be laughed off by both parties. In business, however, you want to do as much as possible to avoid such mishaps.

When cultures collide, as they inevitably will, the damage can be greatly reduced with knowledge, understanding and appreciation of what caused the collision.

Passport Japan

This book will introduce you to Japan's business culture, offer some insights into the country and its people and help you understand how the local traditions, etiquette, values and communication styles differ from your own.

It is, however, only a beginning. Success will come from continuous learning through books and personal experience. This knowledge will make both your business and social transactions smoother and more enjoyable for everyone involved.

JAPAN
Quick Look

Official name	Nippon (Nihon)
Land area	377,835 sq km
Capital & largest city	Greater Tokyo, 12 million
Elevations	Highest–Mount Fuji 3,776 m
	Lowest–sea level along coast

People
Population (1995)	125,506,492
Density	332 persons per sq km
Distribution (1994)	77% urban, 23% rural
Annual growth (1995)	.32%

Official language	Japanese
Major religions	Buddhism, Shinto

Economy (1994)
GDP	US$2.5274 trillion
	US$20,200 per capita
Foreign trade	Imports — US$274.3 billion
	Exports — US$395.5 billion
	Surplus — US$121.2 billion
Principal trade partners	Southeast Asia 29.7%
	USA 26.5%
	Western Europe 16.7%
	China 6.6%
Currency Exch. (1995)	105.2 yen = US$1

Education and health
Literacy (1995)	99%
Universities (1993)	534
Hospital beds (1991)	1 per 448 persons
Physicians (1989)	1 per 2,095 persons
Life expectancy (1995)	Women — 82.4 years
	Men — 76.6 years
Infant mortality (1995)	4.3 per 1,000 live births

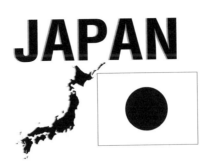

JAPAN

2   Country Facts

Japan is made up of more than 3,000 islands extending NE to SW in eastern Asia between the Pacific Ocean and the Sea of Japan. Four large islands (Honshu, Hokkaido, Shikoku and Kyushu) account for 98 percent of the land area and are home to virtually all of the population. Although Japan's total land mass is somewhat larger than Germany, Japan's 125 million residents live on the 16 percent that is level.

By the year 1700, Edo (now Tokyo) was the largest city in the world; today, it has an estimated population of eight million. The Tokyo-Osaka-Nagoya metropolitan area is home to 45 percent of the population. Overall, 80 percent of Japanese live in urban areas.

The people are 99.4 percent Japanese with Koreans accounting for almost all the remaining .06 percent. The vast majority of Japanese (84 percent) observe both Shinto and Buddhist rites; approximately two percent practice Christianity.

Climate

Japan stretches 3,000 km (1,875 miles) from Sakhalin Island in the north to Sakishima Island, southwest of Okinawa — equivalent to the distance between Seville and Stockholm, or between Maine and Miami. That longitudinal expanse, augmented by precipitous mountain ranges which occupy 80 percent of its area, creates a climate that runs the gamut from sub-arctic (in Hokkaido) to sub-tropical (in Okinawa) and is fairly mild in between.

Most of the main island (Honshu) has sunny winters. Tokyo's January temperatures are comparable to those in London or Washington, DC; any snow soon melts into slush. Shikoku and Kyushu winters are a little milder, while Hokkaido and northern Honshu have severe winters with heavy snows.

Summers are humid, rainy, and warm throughout the islands. High temperatures in Tokyo hover around 31°C (8°F) and occasionally reach 35°C (95°F) — about the same as in central Europe. Japan is in the track of Pacific summer typhoons, so take any radio and television warnings seriously. As in the rest of East Asia, spring and fall are especially pleasant, with warm days, cool nights and fresh breezes.

Business Hours

Normal business hours are from 9 A.M. to 5 P.M. Monday through Friday (with a noon-to-1 P.M. lunch break) and from 9 A.M. to noon every Saturday or on alternate Saturdays. Banks are open from 9 A.M. to 3 P.M. on weekdays. Stores and shops are open from 10 A.M. to 8 P.M., although department stores generally close by 7 P.M.. Many large stores are closed on Wednesday or Thursday but remain open on Saturday and Sunday.

National Holidays

New Year*...................................January 1–3
Adults' Day*................................January 15
National Foundation Day* ....February 11
Spring Equinox* ....around March 21
Golden Week*............................April 29–May 5
Constitution Day* ....May 3
Children's Day* ....May 5
Obon (Festival of Souls) ....August 13–16
Respect for the Aged Day* ....September 15
Autumnal Equinox* ....usually September 23
Health-Sports Day*......................October 10
Culture Day*...............................November 3
Labor-Thanksgiving Day*..........November 23
Emperor's Birthday* ....December 23
Christmas..................................December 25
Osho-Gatsu ....December 27

*Paid Legal Holiday

During most legal holidays, it's very difficult to conduct business. Even if many businesspeople come to the office during these holidays, do not expect them to reach any decisions. Because Japanese offices usually make decisions as a group, all of the members usually need to be present before a decision is finalized.

You also don't want to take a vacation during these times. Japanese vacation destinations are so crowded, especially during Golden Week, that 100 km traffic jams are not uncommon. Be aware that planes leaving Japan for common overseas destinations such as Korea or Hawaii are fully booked almost a year in advance.

3   The Japanese

Language

A number of factors have combined to make Japanese a domestic rather than an international language. These factors include the linguistic remoteness of Japanese from other major languages, the staggering complexity of its written form (basic literacy requires mastery of two phonetic alphabets, approximately 2000 pictograms, plus Roman characters), and the relatively small number of non-native speakers who have mastered it. (During the American occupation of Japan, General Douglas MacArthur ordered that the number of characters be reduced by half to make Japanese more accessible to the peasantry.)

The many spoken dialects of Japanese are more or less mutually intelligible, with the Tokyo dialect acting as the standard for textbooks, media, and business.

The Japanese have applied many characters from the Chinese written language to their own, with the result that Japanese and Chinese can understand each other's writings, though they cannot generally speak or understand the other's spoken language.

While Japanese has absorbed tens of thousands of foreign words (mostly English), these may have completely different meanings and pronunciations. *Handoru*, for example, comes from the English word handle, but it means steering wheel.

The Japanese are voracious readers. They have the highest per capita newspaper readership in the industrialized world, double the rate of the U.S. Perhaps the most interesting side to the Japanese reading appetite is the proliferation of *manga* (comic books); about a billion are sold annually. They range in subject matter from stories about the Tokyo stock exchange to samurai sagas to blatant pornography. It is not unusual to see both school children and middle-aged businessmen reading them on their morning commutes.

Japan's global economic success, combined with dramatic advances in worldwide communications and media, has resulted in a new emphasis on learning English; still, as a general rule, it's mostly younger Japanese who can converse in it. Don't be surprised, however, if they suddenly "forget" their Western language skills in the presence of older or more senior Japanese. To show superior knowledge under such circumstances is considered immodest and disrespectful.

The Self, Group and Authority

Japan's feudal era left an indelible mark on the culture; since then, Japanese identity, honor and, in some ways, survival have depended on membership in (and protection by) the local groups to which people belong. Today, the Japanese see themselves in terms of family, village, religion, university, company, ethnicity, etc.

They associate being part of (and dependent on) a group as a sign of maturity. Without a group affiliation, a Japanese feels very vulnerable and is likely to have difficulty fitting in. *Ippiki ookami* (lone wolves) are considered selfish and untrustworthy. This is the opposite of Western culture, wherein maturity is associated with independence and individualism.

Group behavior is reinforced both in the classroom and in society. And while college students do receive some freedom, the dual institutions of company and marriage usually squash out most remaining individualism. (The phrase *derukuri wa utareru* — "the nail that sticks out is hammered down" — is well known in Japan.) It's been noted that today's adolescent Japanese act more independently than their parents; but it's also true that many of them choose to express their individuality in groups (see note on the recent "tea hair" trend in Chapter 18).

One's place *within* the group is also extremely important. Rarely do individuals approach a relationship as equals. If one is older (and, therefore, the authority figure) or more prominent in the business hierarchy, or of a higher educational or social status, he is treated with the respect due to such a position, regardless of his talents or abilities. This recognition of status is also evident in the Japanese language, where one uses a different vocabulary depending on one's place in relation to the person being addressed.

This can be witnessed in public. When two people are meeting for the first time, one may make a low bow and a polite self-introduction, but upon some hint from the other (for example, seeing a title on a business card, or hearing a manner of speaking) begin a lower bow and a more humble speech pattern. To a non-Japanese, what may seem like a ridiculous amount of bowing is many times an exercise in finding one's place.

An Absence of Privacy

The practice of subordination to group needs, combined with the extreme population density, has resulted in an absence of individual privacy. In fact, the language has no word for "privacy."

Japanese have learned to live as if those around them were not there. Paper walls are somehow soundproof, and close neighbors focus on their miniature gardens, ignoring the other's proximity. Wedged face-to-face in a subway car, Japanese will only acknowledge someone they already know. Strangers, in effect, don't exist. The fastest way for someone in difficulty to be helped in such a situation is to turn to the nearest person and speak directly to them. This rare occurrence immediately alerts the other that something out of the ordinary is happening.

The Japanese solution for young couples living with their extended families is called the love hotel. About 35,000 of these gaudy edifices — with names like Hotel Candy Box, Palace Versailles and UFO (shaped like a huge saucer with lights that flash in sequence) — can be found across Japan. Guests park in one-car garages (which conceal their license plates) and check in by exchanging money and keys through a slot beneath a covered window, so that no eye contact can be made. The interiors are filled with mirrors, "blue" movies and condoms.

While these hotels are purported get-aways for young marrieds, their peak business hours are between noon and 1 P.M. and from 5 P.M. to 7 P.M. — lunchtime and just after work. Draw your own conclusions.

Respect for Age

The Japanese have a great respect for age and tend to see it as a companion of wisdom. And experience is usually valued over expertise. Many Japanese find it very strange, for example, that Westerners go to a younger doctor or other professional because they think that person has more up-to-date knowledge.

Elders, both in family and in business, are listened to and followed, not only because of Confucian tradition, but also because it's taken as self-evident that they are wiser and more experienced. From time to time, the Japanese government publicly recognizes this cultural attitude by honoring select individuals as "living treasures" — men and women who have devoted their lives to mastering such crafts as sword-making and traditional textile design.

When meeting older Japanese, regardless of their station in life or the context of the encounter, be especially respectful.

How the Japanese View Themselves

The Japanese see themselves as a people who are concerned about others, and whose business decisions take into account the personal needs of their associates and employees.

Harmony always takes precedence over individual desires. Accordingly, the Japanese value the ability to maintain an outward appearance of peace and unity even when the actual situation has neither. They rarely break ranks, and they certainly never do so with foreigners.

Gaijin

The Japanese word for foreigners is *gaijin* (literally, "outside persons"). No matter how closely you develop your relationships with Japanese associates and friends, it is unlikely that you will forget for very long that you are a foreigner. Certainly, the Japanese will never forget. No amount of love and respect for Japan or time spent there will change this. Japanese identify an expatriate first as a foreigner, then as a businessperson, and only then, if at all, as a friend.

This attitude also applies to the Ainu (an indigenous, bearded people who live mainly on the northern island of Hokkaido), who are considered "dark-skinned" and less-than-Japanese. Although the Korean culture is parallel to Japan's in many ways, Koreans are almost universally disdained. Interestingly, both sides consider each other the lowest form of life on the earth. Koreans whose families have lived in Japan for generations are routinely discriminated against, regardless of how successful they may be, and it's very difficult for them to become citizens.

Most Japanese regard Western foreigners with a mixture of fear, awe, fascination, and repulsion. Since such contradictory and confusing emotions are detrimental to harmonious relations, many avoid close contact with foreigners altogether. The best course of action is to spend the time together with your Japanese counterparts asking questions, stressing similarities and participating in the culture as much as possible. The Japanese have invested a considerable amount of time learning Western culture and language; to bridge the gap, non-Japanese need to reciprocate.

Beliefs About Westerners

Some common Japanese perceptions of Westerners are:

- They grow up wealthy and lack the toughness that comes from deprivation.
- They're creative, but do not work well in teams.

- They're motivated, but lack patience.
- They make friends quickly, but their expressions of friendship are often insincere.
- They're selfish and unappreciative of different cultures and ways of doing things.
- Western businesses care more about products than they do about their associates and employees.

Because French products have been widely admired in Japan for decades, the French are somewhat revered. The Germans are particularly respected as business associates, because their values regarding time, precision and efficiency are seen as mirroring Japanese values.

Japanese ambivalence about foreigners constitutes an informal but very real trade barrier for outsiders wishing to enter the Japanese market. But it can be overcome by understanding Japanese values and expectations. A foreigner with a sincere desire to work in Japan, who can adapt to the culture, and who is very patient, will probably succeed.

How Others View the Japanese

After the bombing of Pearl Harbor and the horrors of World War II, much of the West viewed the Japanese as cold, calculating and somewhat overzealous in their nationalism; their Pacific Rim neighbors, on both sides of the water, saw them as simply barbarous. Many Koreans who were alive during the Japanese occupation learned Japanese, but today they would rather starve than speak it. The strange exception to this is Taiwan (then called Formosa) where the invading Japanese were admired for removing the mainland Chinese from power.

The Japanese are generally viewed as people who can copy or improve on existing technologies but are unable to create anything new. This is often attributed to their educational system, which teaches by rote. However, as Japan continues to assert its economic prowess and participate in international peacekeeping and humanitarian programs, many of these stereotypes are being proved wrong.

The Japanese are still generally thought to be secretive and clannish, and there is a prevalent feeling that they put up "unfair" barriers to outsiders wishing to do business in their country.

As hosts, they have a well-documented reputation for graciousness and excellent customer service. Individual Japanese are almost unfailingly polite and willing to go considerably out of their way to be of help.

National Identity and Pride

An island nation with very little immigration in recorded history, Japan developed into one of the most culturally homogeneous countries in the world. As a result, the Japanese have a very keen sense of who is Japanese and who is not. Their long-standing cultural beliefs put a high value on cooperation, discipline, self-control and harmony, and these values reinforce their national, racial and ethnic identity. Though they originally imported their writing system, early political structure, Confucian customs and Buddhism from 6th century China, they managed to make them "Japanese."

And while the postwar Japanese reputation for kindness to foreign visitors (especially Westerners) is well deserved, it is virtually impossible for a foreign national to ever "become" Japanese. A person is either Japanese or *gaijin*, and no amount of study, time or effort will change that. For longtime residents, this can be a source of frustration and disappointment.

4 Cultural Stereotypes

A visitor's perceptions of Japan and the Japanese may be based on personal experience, on what others have said or on stereotypes. These perceptions are almost certain to color both your social and business relationships. Those based on personal experience or valid research will probably be useful. Outdated or inaccurate information will create barriers.

While stereotypes vary, some are common.

Work-Obsessed

The Japanese dedicate their lives to work and their company.

It is true that Japan reconstructed its shattered economy after World War II in an astonishingly short period by dedicating itself almost entirely to industrial production. Employees were expected to work long hours, six or seven days a week.

In the past decade, the workday has been shortened, and most employees enjoy at least a day and a half off each week. Still, old habits die hard. Many Japanese executives feel that taking vacations shows disloyalty to both their companies and their peers. Vacations of over a week are very rare, and no one on the management track ever uses all of their allotted vacation time. A few companies have gone so far as to make vacations mandatory and to forbid overtime on one day of the week.

After years of hard and incessant work, one of the most common dilemmas for Japanese executives is, "What should I do with my leisure time?" For husbands and wives who haven't seen much of each others in years, "leisure stress" is often sighted as a reason for Japan's increasing divorce rate.

Holidays abroad have become common. Golf courses and weekend resorts have sprung up along Japan's coast and in the mountains. Tennis and *beisu booru* (baseball) are popular, and Japan has more ski resorts than the United States.

Not Creative

Japan's industrial growth was spurred by copying and improving upon designs created by others, and then producing them more efficiently.

While this is partly true, Japan's production methods and its refinement of existing designs have reached a level that can only be called innovative. During the past decade, they have proved themselves to be world-class leaders in the fields of high technology, robotics and pharmaceuticals, and their quality, productivity and management models are emulated worldwide.

Blind Obedience

The Japanese exercise blind obedience both to tradition and to authority.

Obedience is indeed a part of Confucianism, which influences every aspect of Japanese life and teaches that it is not appropriate to question authority or undermine group harmony.

However, a new generation of Japanese is coming to power. Often having been schooled in the West, they do not hesitate to assert themselves or question tradition. Their influence will become much more apparent as they begin to assert themselves as managers.

Stoic and Unemotional

The Japanese, especially Japanese men, are stoic and unemotional.

Feeling emotion and displaying it publicly are two different things. Japanese are taught from an early age to mask their emotions, hide their disappointments, refrain from overt displays of either anger or joy, and above all, not cry in public. (And children are often told that they should or should not do something "because people will laugh.") Displaying emotion, even in front of other Japanese, is thought to draw unnecessary and unwelcome attention to oneself.

Chauvinistic

The Japanese are extremely chauvinistic, both in their nationalism and in their attitudes toward women.

The Japanese take great pride in their country, their heritage and their traditions, and they have a tendency to look down on foreign ways. However, as Japanese business extends its influence further afield, they have come to accept and even appreciate some aspects of foreign cultures.

The Japanese have been forced to revise their attitudes toward (and treatment of) women in response to both the rising educational level of Japanese women and their increasing participation in the work force. Female tourists and visiting businesswomen will experience extreme politeness and deference — which is more likely chivalry than chauvinism.

Regional Differences

Because of the homogeneity of its population, Japan has fewer regional differences than many countries. Distinctions based on race, ethnicity, tribe, religion or language don't, for the most part, apply. However, the Japanese take pride in their distinct regional foods, festivals, dress, customs and products.

The Kansai region (which includes Osaka) has its own way of doing business; residents here are adamant in proclaiming their acumen over other Japanese, particularly those from Tokyo. The traditional Osaka greeting, *"Mookarimakka?,"* translates into English as, "Are you making a lot of money?" The old capital of Kyoto is famous for its thousands of temples, and it's home to one of few remaining geisha districts.

The usual observations can be made about the contrast between the fast pace and isolation of urban existence and the more traditional, community-oriented rural life. It's said that cities like Tokyo and Osaka are not the "real" Japan. But with Kanto (Tokyo-Yokohama area), Chubu (Nagoya) and the Kansai corridor (Osaka-Kyoto-Kobe area) making up 60 percent of Japan's population, it's difficult to discount them as unreal.

6   Government & Business

The collaborative relationship between the Japanese government and business is among the strongest in the world. Since the end of World War II, the government has supported the rebuilding of the economy through financial and banking incentives, development consortiums, *gyosei shido* (administrative guidance) and sponsored research. And though Japan already spends a larger percentage of its gross domestic product (GDP) on the aforementioned research than any other country in the world, the government has recently committed itself to doubling that figure.

Barriers to Trade and Competition

In addition to creating an environment where business can thrive, the government has long sought to protect Japanese businesses from foreign competition by such informal practices as restrictive distribution and licensing agreements, financial pressure on distributors and retailers, and complex registration procedures and requirements.

While formal barriers to trade, such as tariffs and overt discrimination, are almost all gone, the highly developed structure of the Japanese economy makes it difficult for newcomers to compete. But as usual, when an economy is protected and too highly structured, niches and cracks appear — and as exemplified by the success of such innovative companies as Amway (consumer goods), Domino's Pizza, Starbucks Coffee and Apple Computer.

The Iron Triangle

Alliances between big business, Japanese ministries and politicians are often referred to as the Iron Triangle. This three-way relationship was probably the principal cause of the recent setbacks suffered by the long-dominant Liberal Democratic Party (LDP). Until recently, support for a political party and its candidates — in the form of large contributions, informal agreements between a government agency and a particular company, and special consideration for favored legislation — were all common aspects of "doing business."

Probably the most powerful members of the Japanese government are the bureaucrats of the 12 national ministries. While the word "bureaucrat" in most cultures implies a petty and obstructive official, the position in Japan is highly revered. Only the top two percent from the top four universities join the ministries. These bureaucrats are over worked, underpaid and very powerful, and in most cases, they're able to easily overpower the Japanese Prime Minister and parliament.

Most prestigious and powerful of all is the Ministry of Finance (MoF), through its control of the government budget. Next is the Ministry of International Trade and Industry (MITI) which is often credited with engineering the Japanese economic miracle. (The turf battles between ministries are intense.)

Recent events concerning Japanese bank regulation have highlighted two aspects of the government bureaucracy with regard to business.

First, government agencies are so large and complex that it's even difficult for people within them to understand what's going on. The business of licensing, permits, compliance, visas and clearances can be impenetrable (or, at the very least, costly and time-consuming) for most foreigners. The only hope is an alliance with someone in the government, or more probably with a Japanese specialist in government-business affairs.

Second, the Japanese do not like to "air their dirty laundry" in public. This was especially apparent in the failure of Japanese financial regulators to promptly notify their U.S. government counterparts of irregularities in Daiwa Bank's U.S. operations. The conventional wisdom is that the government will quietly intervene (in ways that are often surprising to Western observers) to clean up or eliminate a problem before it becomes widely known.

Insiders and Outsiders

Put simply, those inside the system benefit from it; those outside have little opportunity to manipulate (let alone penetrate) it, and they stand little chance of obtaining favors. Business offers lucrative positions to bureaucrats who retire from the government, and the rate of transfer of government bureaucrats to private companies is rising.

Former bureaucrats serve on the boards of 23 percent of Japan's major companies, despite restrictions on accepting positions in industries that they previously regulated. Interestingly, even many foreign companies have learned how to play the game and have become successful at recruiting former Japanese bureaucrats to their boards.

 The Work Environment

Lifetime Commitment

The traditional job in Japan requires a lifelong commitment in return for a career of predictable promotions and increasing benefits. Promotions are based not so much on merit or accomplishment as on an employee's age and length of tenure.

Traditionally, management practices focus on long-term development. Employees are neither hired nor fired on the basis of their ability to aggressively produce short-term results. In fact, laying off an employee is seen as a disgrace for all parties concerned. Until very recently, top companies only did so in the face of great financial difficulty.

However, this approach is increasingly giving way to the realities of the world marketplace. Employees are no longer assured lifetime employment, and companies find that they must compete to attract and keep "talent." While some huge conglomerates retain traditional promotion systems, many companies are now trying to base pay raises and promotions on an individual's particular ability and contribution (albeit with very limited success).

In major companies, changing jobs is almost unheard of. The company becomes both one's work

group and social group. In many cases, there are
also financial and housing ties. The reputation of
one's company can give instant credit at restaurants
(just by passing a business card to the cashier) or
can serve as an irrefutable reference when seeking
an apartment. Separation from the company would
mean a life change, not just a job change.

Those Who Sit By the Window

After they are recruited from universities,
newly hired employees in large companies are
expected to follow a prescribed path. Until the age
of about 45, they will be trained and educated in
the company ways and rotated from one area or
location to another. Then, a decision is made as to
whether they should be promoted to the position of
a company director. If so, they can then work well
beyond the normal retirement age, perhaps even
into their eighties. If not, they are expected to retire
at 55. Those reluctant to retire are shunted aside to
become *madogiwazoku*, or "those who sit by the
window."

Assignments Abroad

An overseas posting is a dilemma for a Japanese executive. The plus sides are many, often
including an expatriate expense package that
allows a standard of living unheard of in Japan, the
prestige of being picked for an overseas assignment, and a chance to experience another country.

On the other hand, many companies insist that
those assigned to foreign posts be married; wives
are expected to drop whatever they're doing to
accompany their husbands. It's relatively easy to
bring younger children overseas, but older (particularly male) children usually stay in Japan so as not

to lose their place in the race to enter a prestigious university.

Many executives stationed overseas loose *jimyaku* (personal connections), which are what Japanese companies look for in their top executives. This can be particularly problematic when the overseas assignment has ended and the executive returns home.

Seniority and Status

In ancient Japan, every person was categorized as belonging to a distinct class based upon family background and occupation. The lowest were the menial laborers, the highest included the Emperor and his family. Within each class, there was another ranking system, often with the youngest and least skilled people in a particular occupation at the bottom and the oldest (presumably the most skilled and experienced) at the top.

This structure, based on the tenets of Confucianism, remains the basis of Japanese society. The words *sempai* (senior) and *kohai* (junior) are used to express hierarchical relationships in both business and education. Everyone assumes that senior graduates of top universities (Tokyo, Keio and Waseda) will mentor and try to ensure the success of their junior alumnae within a company.

Businessmen in Japan are so concerned about status that they cannot be sure how to behave at an initial meeting until everyone's relative status has been established. For this reason, they exchange name cards before bowing. If the name cards are too vague, they may ask each other about company position, seniority and alma mater. If they miss the appropriate level of humility based on the new knowledge they've received, they may start over and re-bow.

Education

Even if a person is from a well-known and powerful family, he will nominally still be junior to any group members who graduated from a more prestigious university or who graduated before him. In the event that two employees in the same work environment have nearly identical credentials, their rank will be determined by their ability to make personal connections.

The Japanese Work Ethic

Loyalty to the company is seen as an extension of loyalty to the family, so conflict between the two — which is common in Western cultures — is almost nonexistent in Japan.

Although Japanese are reluctant to take individual credit or praise, they are driven by a strong sense of shame and will take responsibility for work "failures" that are beyond their direct control, or for situations from which their counterparts in many cultures would be distancing themselves. An example would be the resignation of the president of an airline because one of its planes crashed on the other side of the world.

Relationships between labor and management, and between blue collar and white collar, tend to be harmonious rather than adversarial. Individuals don't generally compete. However, the Japanese are fiercely competitive team players, both within their own company and against rival companies. Japanese management techniques are designed to harness this competitive spirit; workers are often organized into teams that try to out-produce each other.

Individual employees will rarely act on their own and almost never against the will of the group. Thus, it's both foolish and a waste of time to say to a Japanese business contact, in effect, "Look, if you work with me on this, it will do you a lot of good in your company." Nothing could be further from the truth, and such a ploy is not likely to gain you favor. And as the group often shares in both successes and failures, commission sales designed to reward individuals may cause alienation of the person they're intended to reward.

Decision Making

Traditionally, decision making in Japanese business was a long, time-consuming process. Things are changing in today's fast-moving economy, but long turn-around times are still normal, particularly in larger companies. In theory, decisions include almost every employee involved in the endeavor under discussion and cannot be completed without consensus. While strategic planning and policy making take into consideration the desires of upper management, decisions are often influenced from the bottom up. Ideally, they are then articulated and implemented with resources provided from the top down. "No" is hardly ever an acceptable response to a request from a superior or group, and when unavoidable, it comes in the form of an apparent "yes."

Foreigners managing Japanese employees need to accept the upward flow of decisions as fundamental and learn how to participate in the system. Authoritative management styles are certain to meet with resistance and create ill will.

Ringi-Sho

An important decision usually begins as a suggestion from a *kacho* (middle-level manager) or group of managers. Then it's circulated in written form (known as *ringi-sho* or "project proposal") among all those whom it may affect. Those who approve affix their personal seal to the document, then pass it on to other persons of equal or higher rank. The suggestion gains credibility as seals of approval accumulate. Individuals may suggest modifications. In the end, if there is sufficient support, the *ringi-sho* will be forwarded up to the board of directors. A suggestion that makes it that far is usually authorized for implementation.

Shakun

With a fervor that might be seen by Westerners as almost childlike, Japanese employees repeat what they call *shaken* (slogans). A typical example of these can be seen in the seven principles that are reaffirmed on a daily basis by employees of the Matsushita Electric Company:

1. National Service Through Industry
2. Fairness
3. Harmony and Cooperation
4. Struggle for Betterment
5. Courtesy and Humility
6. Adjustment and Assimilation
7. Gratitude

Most successful foreign companies in Japan have made considerable efforts to translate, publicize and commit their employees to their mission statement. Masami Atarashi, the former President of Johnson & Johnson Japan, often remarks during lectures that committing his former company's employees to a previously forgotten mission statement was the crucial step that pushed the Japanese subsidiary's accounts into the black, after years of bleeding red.

8 Women in Business

Traditional Roles

Historically, Japanese have believed that it is in the best interest of their families and their nation for women to devote themselves to being wives and mothers. In most households, women are responsible for the family budget (with men commonly complaining that their wives don't give them enough allowance) and for making decisions about the education and disciplining of children. They also take responsibility — and public blame — for problems that family members may have.

The majority of Japanese women still believe that marriage and family are the ideals to which they should aspire. There is also a strong belief that the attention given by Japanese women to their families has led to the low level of delinquency and good classroom behavior of Japanese children, compared with the children of dual-income families in the West.

Changing Trends

The labor shortages of the 1980s inspired an unprecedented influx of women into the Japanese

workplace. To date, they've gained the most accep-
tance in production and service industries, but their
pay remains significantly lower, in many cases,
than that of their male counterparts. It's not uncommon for young working women to be referred to as
office "flowers" and to be expected to quit when
they marry. Help-wanted ads often specify the sex
of employees sought and set an age limit for female
applicants.

Many women still hesitate to assert themselves
professionally for fear of offending their more traditional families, boyfriends or husbands. However,
Japanese businessmen are beginning to recognize
that women in the West hold high-level positions in
business and government and have adjusted their
expectations and behavior to some degree.

Recently, many young Japanese women have
rejected both the idea of early marriage and of climb-
ing the corporate ladder. Having observed their
older male counterparts endure years of drudgery
and overtime for the vague promise of rewards in
the far future, they're happy to simply take their sal-
aries, bonuses and full vacation time and leave work
at five o'clock.

Avoiding "Foreign Intervention"

It's important to understand that the business
arena is not an appropriate forum in which to express
political views regarding woman's rights or to
attempt to show the Japanese the error of their ways.

Such behavior will serve only to embarrass the
Japanese on your behalf and create a level of discomfort almost certain to ensure failure of purpose.
Social changes are slow in coming in Japan, and
they are internally driven.

Strategies for Western Businesswomen

A female team leader can make it abundantly clear that she is in charge by putting her name at the top of a list of team members, by including more biographical information on herself than on other members, and by emphasizing her credentials and accomplishments.

She can ensure that the Japanese do not ignore her status by instructing her team to defer to her all questions directed to others that should appropriately go to her. Perhaps most important, her team should refrain from disagreeing or engaging in a "brainstorming" session in front of the Japanese.

Foreign businesswomen should not expect to be included in the evening business activities and should not be offended if they are not. The Japanese business-entertainment industry simply hasn't had a great deal of experience catering to women, and they don't know how to entertain them.

This doesn't have to be detrimental and can be turned into a tool. As the senior manager, a businesswoman has a chance to politely bow out of a drinking session and then suggest a male associate attend instead. Provide the associate with a specific agenda of items for feeling out Japanese counterparts, maybe a modified version of the good cop/bad cop strategy. The informal setting will provide a venue to push agendas, test limits, smooth over rough points or mistakes from a previous meeting, test new proposals or engage in a variety of other similar activities.

If you are included, however, count it as a plus and enjoy yourself.

9 Making Connections

Cultivating Relationships Is Key

The Japanese place tremendous value on personal relationships in their business dealings. This point cannot be overemphasized. Foreigners often fail to establish long-term ties in Japan simply because they do not take the time to earn the trust and respect of their Eastern counterparts.

There are few, if any, ways to shorten the process. And be advised that the Japanese are very skilled at recognizing superficiality, haste and what they consider to be a lack of respect. While they may never say "no," they will hesitate to move forward if they feel that a genuine rapport has not been established.

A number of personal visits to your prospective associates is mandatory, and there will be little apparent progress or tangible results for quite some time. Although some agreements and contracts can be made within a year, foreign companies that have firmly established themselves in Japan report that the process took a number of years. Budget accordingly.

When starting out in Japan, most executives try to make their trips as quickly (and cheaply) as possible. However, it's very difficult to learn about a large and complex market like Japan when on the run, especially given today's tighter-than-ever schedules. And such behavior is likely to be interpreted as a lack of commitment by your Japanese counterparts.

The Go-Between

"Cold" calls and unsolicited marketing materials are not good business strategies in Japan. The best course is to find a *chukaisha* (mutual friend or connection) who can introduce you to prospective customers and give assurances about your reputation and business acumen.

A Japanese will probably not do business with you until he has had time to develop a sense of your ethics and intentions. In fact, he will sometimes avoid meeting with a stranger altogether, until someone he knows (usually also Japanese) introduces you. Remember that the *chukaisha* is, in effect, loaning you his reputation and that people, companies, organizations and schools extend constant, tremendous effort over a period of years to build and keep a reputation. Considering this, it's not surprising that unless a potential connection knows you very well, you may receive an excuse instead of an introduction.

If you can't identify a *chukaisha*, you may be able to get a bank or other company to introduce you as a reliable client of theirs. For years, large Japanese companies have employed retired government officials, well-known Japanese political figures, and others of prominent stature to act as go-betweens (*komon* or *sodan-yaku*). Western companies, especially those seeking strategic partnerships, should consider this strategy as money well spent.

Beware. There are lots of so-called consultants

who claim to know all of the "key" players; in many cases, these are limited to companies or executives the consultant knows, and they may not always make the best possible partners. And if your *chukaisha*'s reputation is not good, or his contacts do not pick up your project, you can find yourself in a bind.

Many times, a good consultant is necessary to shorten learning curves and avoid costly mistakes, but it is advisable and prudent to get a second or third opinion and then personally verify your findings, as well as the reputation of your *chukaisha*.

Written Introductions

Before attempting to meet with representatives of a Japanese company, you should arrange for *shokai-jo* (letters of introduction) from well-known business leaders, overseas Japanese, or former government officials who have dealt with Japan. The usual procedure is for your reference to write a letter directly to the person whom you want to meet, asking him to give you special consideration. Written introductions are most effective if they come from a high-ranking executive in a company with which your target company does business or from a close family friend of the person you want to meet.

Although *shokai-jo* are less effective than the personal introduction by a go-between, they can pave the way for an initial meeting. As in the case of the go-between, the person who writes your letters of introduction should, ideally, be Japanese.

If you represent a smaller company and cannot get high-level introductions, all is not lost; it does, however, usually take more effort. As a foreigner, you may not have to play by all the Japanese rules. If you don't have someone to vouch for your reputation, you must make the attempt yourself. This may include repeated business trips to Japan, attendance at industry trade shows, extending invitations to Japanese to visit you at trade shows in your own country, and the creation of corporate materials that emphasize your company's reputation (as opposed to its products).

Always keep in mind that persistence and patience are highly valued in Japan. *Ishi no ue nimo san nen* — you must have the patience to sit on a rock for three years in order to warm it.

Common Japanese Business Titles

Since status is largely determined by title in Japan, the Japanese will appreciate it if your title matches something they are familiar with. There is a tendency by foreign managers to directly translate their titles into Japanese via phonetic spelling; nothing will confuse your Japanese counterparts more. After having your title translated, always have it checked by a native speaker. On the next page is a listing of common Japanese business titles.

Japanese Business Titles

Japanese	English Translation	Usual Seniority	Typical Age Range
Kaicho	Chairman	40 years or more	60+
Shacho	President	40 years or more	60+
Senmu Torishima-riyaku	Senior Managing Director	40 years or more	60+
Jomu Torishima-riyaku	Executive Managing Director	40 years or more	60+
Torishima-riyaku	Director	35 years or more	55+
Bucho	General Manager	25 years or more	late 40s
Bucho Dairi	Deputy General Manager	25 years or more	late 40s
Kacho	Section Chief	17–27 years	40-50
Kakaricho	Assistant Section Chief	11–20 years	33–43
No Title	Assistant Clerk, etc.	8–10 years	23–33

10 Strategies for Success

Establish Relationships

Take the time to get acquainted with your Japanese peers and to establish respect and trust. Wait patiently at each meeting and business-social gathering for signs that your rapport is increasing. Do not expect to come home from the first (or second or third) trip with a deal. Relationships are paramount in Japan.

If you should break a relationship, no matter how logical the reasons, you will always be seen as a typical unreliable foreigner. Don't burn bridges, and always put the best face-saving slant on the story, regardless of what really happened. It will earn you respect and assure others that you're conscious of their circumstances.

Find a Matchmaker

Find someone who can introduce you to the right people in the target company. Third-party introductions, especially by Japanese, are extremely important for making initial contacts and creating first impressions. A go-between not only introduces you, but is often involved in negotiations until the deal is closed (and sometimes beyond). In Japan a matchmaker is commonly asked to ease tensions in times of trouble.

Be Calm and Cordial

Japanese are more concerned with maintaining harmony and avoiding embarrassment than they are with achieving higher sales and profits. This doesn't mean that they're not interested in monetary success, just that they prefer to achieve it under harmonious circumstances.

Aim High at the Beginning

Approach a Japanese organization at the highest level possible. It's likely that you won't meet with the senior executive at first, but the fact that he was the contact means that he will be involved and kept apprised from the beginning.

Use Both Sides of Your Brain

Don't rely solely on logic and persuasion to make your case. The Japanese are not "logical" or *dorai* ("dry") in the usual Western sense. Although they value a thoughtful, cognitive and intellectual approach, they also consider intuition, instinct and emotion to be important factors in business.

The Japanese are, in fact, very concerned with the conditions and feelings of others. When they consider you a friend, or when they have decided to include you in their circle, they will act with much more sensitivity and compassion than is usual in Western business.

Keep It Formal

Always maintain an air of formality in your business dealings with Japanese. Seniority and roles should be sharply defined, and your team should always present a united front.

Don't Criticize or Complain

In a group setting, never refer to a failure on the part of a Japanese who is present or of one of their colleagues who is not. And never put a Japanese in a position where he must admit failure. In general, criticism and complaints are best handled delicately. If a mistake made by a Japanese business associate is obvious, take the blame on yourself; everyone will admire you for it.

Be Modest

Kenson (modesty) is both a virtue and an indication of good character and breeding. Avoid praising your own abilities, products and services; let your materials or reputation speak for themselves. Japanese virtually always deny the importance of their accomplishments and the level of their expertise. It's considered gracious for others to do the same.

Leave Money Out of It

Unless it is on the agenda, avoid speaking directly about money. Financial details should be left for a later time or worked out by your go-between or subordinates. The relationship comes first, money second.

Keep Your Sense of Humor

Expect inexplicable delays. The thoughts and motivations of your Japanese associates, when they are not simply impenetrable, will seem to contradict their actions. You'll sometimes feel very far from anything that is familiar, and many of your lifelong strategies just won't work. A sense of humor (and of perspective) is essential. The alternative is to suffer a great deal of frustration and anxiety.

11   Time

In Japan, particularly in the business sector, the question is not how much time things take, but when the time will be taken.

Many Westerners will announce a new development or decision as soon as the key players decide to proceed, and then take months or years to implement it. Japanese will take as long as is necessary to gain consensus before announcing a decision, and then immediately implement it. If the Japanese hold a press conference to announce that they have developed a new computer operating system, they will usually unveil it the same day. Westerners, in comparison, will likely have made their announcement months or even years before showing their working prototype.

Deadlines

The Japanese tend to resist any pressure placed on them regarding deadlines or delivery dates, as they can't predict how much time the consensus-gathering process will take. If they seem to agree to a deadline, they may be doing so in order to maintain harmony, not because they expect to meet it.

It may take years to negotiate a joint venture, licensing or distribution agreement, but once the Japanese side has agreed, they will expect immediate action. If the foreign partner is not ready to move, the Japanese will likely accuse him of "endless" delays and procrastination.

Appointments

Traditionally, Japanese were accustomed to meeting both with and without appointments, but the pace of modern business has made appointments the norm.

Being on time is important, but senior executives and other important figures are expected to be five to seven minutes late — to reflect their "busy" schedules. No one, however, should be more than 10 minutes late.

Breakfast meetings are extremely unpopular. In general Japanese offices open at 9 A.M., and workers are expected to be there — at least physically. But constant twelve-hour workdays, commutes averaging an hour and a half each way, and night after night of drinking and singing result in very little work getting accomplished in the morning.

In Tokyo, especially, allow time to compensate for heavy traffic and the possibility that your taxi driver may not know how to find your destination. The layout of the streets in many areas was designed to confuse invading armies, and the address system can be almost incomprehensible. Even Japanese seek out *koban* (small corner police stations) for directions. If you want to tell a taxi driver where to go, mention a famous location near your destination, and the specific address later. Plan no more than three meetings a day. Once you become more familiar with Japan, you may be able to do more, but don't count on it.

 12 **Business Meetings**

Arranging the Meeting

Business meetings, especially ones with a large company, need to be scheduled weeks in advance. Meetings are conducted formally, and Westerners should prepare for them thoroughly. While the Japanese are reluctant to deny a meeting outright, their response may send signals indicating their degree of interest in your offer, or they may send no reply at all if they are not interested.

In setting up a first meeting, it is imperative that you try to meet with people who are on the appropriate levels and can make important decisions. You may meet the boss, but top Japanese executives are often jealously guarded by a host of senior directors and junior executives.

If your delegation includes senior-level executives, Japanese section managers may arrange for a superior to meet with you briefly as a courtesy. The absence of a high-level Japanese counterpart in your first few meetings is not necessarily a bad sign, as business relationships are usually initiated by junior executives. Higher-ranking executives are introduced as the relationship progresses, or at ceremonial functions.

Whomever you see first, even if he is the head of the company, you will still need to meet people on many different levels if you want to ensure good relations. If you don't establish good relations with the middle- and junior-level managers (who are actually going to do the work), they may resent you for having bypassed them.

Preparing the Japanese

Once a meeting has been set, send a hierarchical list of the team members who will be visiting, including their full names, genders (indicated in the "old-fashioned" way by Mr./Mrs./Miss) and titles. Put the team leader's name at the top of the list and include more biographical information, credentials and accomplishments for him or her than for the others. Before the meeting, mail or fax a detailed agenda of the matters to be discussed. This will allow the Japanese time to confer among themselves and to send an appropriate reply. Do not surprise your hosts by bringing an unannounced face to the meeting, particularly if that person is of high rank.

The Role of the Japanese Leader

Many foreign businesspeople have been dismayed because top Japanese executives seem to have little interest in the details of the proposal or project at hand. This is mainly because the role of a Japanese company leader differs from that of their Western counterpart. Japanese senior executives are primarily consensus builders who have risen to their positions as a result of seniority, loyalty, amiability, and their ability to garner trust.

Rarely does a rugged individualist with a flair for cutting deals make it into Japanese leadership circles — that type of person is not well suited to maintaining the sense of harmony, peace and tranquillity so central to the Japanese management style. Don't burden a company head with the intricate details of your plan unless he asks for them. Concentrate on listening carefully and answering his questions thoroughly and sincerely. These questions will likely be about the structure of your company, your experience with the business, and the guiding philosophy of your company's founder.

Determining Who's Who

Sometimes, it's difficult to tell who among the Japanese is the most senior, especially on a first visit. Age and an air of authority are good clues. Studying Japanese business titles is useful, but remember that the English-equivalent titles are not as exacting as the Japanese ones.

Don't be fooled into judgments about a person's importance based on how much he talks. Japanese senior executives are well known for saying little, even to their own colleagues; often, they only utter an occasional word or make a noise to indicate approval or disapproval.

Some senior executives do not speak English as well as their subordinates and may choose not to do so for fear of making mistakes. Others may refuse to converse in English for purely tactical reasons.

Presenting Yourself

Both before and during your visit, state the nature of your business concisely and with confidence. The Japanese are a thorough, orderly people, and the way in which you present yourself is the most important element of the beginning stages of a business relationship.

Typically, Japanese in the business world read English better than they speak or understand it. Speak slowly and clearly, and avoid slang or idioms.

Most importantly, your presentation should take into account the profile of the audience — their positions in the organization and their probable levels of technical expertise.

It's a good idea to translate as much of your presentation material as possible into Japanese. Ideally, you should send a kit of materials to each individual who will be attending the presentation. A typical kit should contain:

- A brochure describing your company
- An overview of your company that includes the names and titles of its top executives, its philosophy, values and mission statement, a list of its products and services, and a short history
- A short biography of the top executive, as well as the leader of your delegation
- Information demonstrating the success of your company in providing the products or services that you're proposing to offer, as well as facts that demonstrate that they are innovative and superior to similar offerings by other companies

During the meeting, your delegation should open the presentation kit and explain its contents. The kits should be undamaged, unsoiled, and carefully packaged in high-quality materials. The Japanese concern with appearance was reflected in a recent air freight survey in which customers reported that they preferred receiving a package in perfect condition to getting it on time.

Do not worry when Japanese executives, particularly senior ones, close their eyes during a meeting. In most cases, they are concentrating, not sleeping.

Meeting Guidelines

1. Your team should enter the room in order of rank, and your team leader should be ready to greet the leader of the Japanese side. He or she should then introduce the Japanese leader to the members of your group in descending order of rank.

2. Exchange name cards, first with the senior Japanese executive, then with his subordinates.

3. Your team leader should open the meeting for your side by presenting the other members and identifying their roles and/or specializations. Remarks should be addressed to the senior member of the Japanese team, who will most likely be seated directly across the table.

4. Establish team protocol in advance to ensure that questions mistakenly addressed to other team members are deferred to your team leader.

5. Don't disagree in the presence of the Japanese team. Save any brainstorming and "devil's advocate" discussions for private meetings.

Concluding the Meeting

As the meeting concludes, your team leader should thank the head of the Japanese group personally and express appreciation for the opportunity to meet.

If appropriate, it's always good to emphasize a desire to establish a long and mutually beneficial relationship. You needn't be as specific with regard to deadlines as you might be in the West. Vagueness and ambiguity are the preferred means of expression.

If possible, your team should say good-bye personally to everyone in the room (again, in descending order of rank). The same guidelines with regard to bowing and/or shaking hands apply.

13 Negotiating with the Japanese

Once you have established a personal relationship, substantive talks can begin. The number of negotiation team members can vary widely, depending on the nature of the business. The Japanese will try to match each of the visitors with a member of their team.

Avoid bringing attorneys to negotiating sessions; the Japanese will interpret their presence on your team as a sign of your distrust.

Formality versus Small Talk

Negotiations are often held in meeting rooms at the Japanese place of business, and the Japanese will probably be already assembled there when you arrive. The head of the visiting delegation should enter the meeting room first. This is Japanese custom. If an interpreter escorts the visiting team, he should enter close behind the leader and remain by the leader's side throughout the negotiations.

After a round of handshakes, bows and smiles, the visitors are seated opposite their Japanese counterparts, with the team leaders sitting directly across from each other at the center of the table. Other team members are often arrayed in descending order of importance. Most likely, the guest delegation will be seated facing the door as a matter of courtesy. Tea or other drinks are provided.

The Japanese are patient people and do not expect to immediately jump into substantive negotiations. "Small talk" is used to establish an initial rapport and to help both sides get a feel for each other.

Opening Protocol

After initial courtesies, the head of the host delegation usually delivers a short welcoming speech, then turns the floor over to the head of the guest delegation. Japanese customarily allow visitors to speak first in negotiations. In some ways, this can be to their advantage, but the participants usually know enough about each other's positions to preclude surprises (the Japanese don't like surprises at the negotiation table). The team leader is looked to for all meaningful dialogue. Conflicting statements from team members will be interpreted as a weakness in position or commitment. Team members should speak only when they are asked to do so by their leader.

Describe your basic positions at the very beginning. It can be useful to distribute sheets summarizing your main points in Japanese. When it is the appropriate time to tackle a business issue, the Japanese appreciate directness. Do what you can to clarify their understanding of your position. In most cases, it's best to begin your presentation with "the big picture" and to wait until later in the talks to discuss specific details.

After the visiting team leader outlines his team's position, the Japanese team leader will respond point by point, noting any perceived omissions. From this point on, the negotiation will run with the rhythm of a controlled conversation, rather than an open-ended chat.

Top Japanese Negotiating Tactics

- Extremely well-prepared and orchestrated team
- Use of long pauses and silences (don't give anything away by filling these in)
- Delayed or ambiguous answers
- Frequent "side conversations" in Japanese
- Use of an interpreter to gain time for thinking
- Change of venue to a more informal setting
- Use of emotional pleas
- Closing "squeeze"

Japanese know that Westerners (especially Americans) are very time conscious. In general, a foreign businessman's trips to Japan are short, and he intends to return home with something accomplished. Japanese may take advantage of this by delaying their decisions until the last minute, forcing the visitor to either accept their position or go home empty-handed.

There are several ways to combat this.

- Don't specify your departure date (and imply that it's earlier than it really is)
- Cushion your departure time so that you can extend your trip if the meeting isn't successfully concluded (then the Japanese will be worried about their own schedules and will want to reach a quick agreement)
- Conclude the meeting as "successful" (surface harmony), agree to follow up, and schedule another meeting in the future. In general, the more you go to Japan, the less the delaying tactic will be deliberately used against you.

Interpreters

Even those Japanese who speak English are not likely to put themselves at a disadvantage by having to negotiate in a foreign tongue. A member of the Japanese delegation will probably act as an interpreter, but it is not advisable to depend on him exclusively. Although there is little risk that he will try to intentionally mislead you, chances are good that he will not understand all the nuances and inferences of English, and he is, after all, a member of their team.

Even someone as experienced as Edwin Reischauer (the first post-World War II U.S. ambassador to Japan and a man who grew up bilingual in Japan) used interpreters, if only to gain time to think about a response as the translation was going on.

Interpreters can be expensive, but they're essential, especially in sensitive high-stakes negotiations. Most Japanese interpreters are women — possibly because women are less afraid of losing face during the years of mistakes that precede becoming bilingual. She should be multicultural as well, able to pick up on feelings and intonations in both languages. Ideally, you will have located an interpreter in advance, but even after you've arrived, your hotel business center can refer you to a service that specializes in providing them.

Tips on Using Interpreters

1.   Establish Guidelines

Before a meeting, discuss the mechanics of how you will work together. (For example, how long should you speak before pausing for interpretation?) Brief your interpreter thoroughly, go over any specialized vocabulary, and provide her with as much written material as possible. Give her time to become familiar with your style, humor and body language. This will help ensure that your messages are conveyed accurately.

2. Don't Exhaust Your Interpreter

During a meeting or negotiating session, stop every few sentences to allow for interpretation, and try to limit each sentence to one main point.

Interpreters should rest at least every two hours. If negotiations continue for more than a day, you may need two interpreters. Using an interpreter can stretch a meeting to three times its normal length, so be patient with the flow of discussion.

3. Address Your Japanese Counterpart

Look toward the head of the Japanese team, not at the interpreter; Japanese value personal communication. They may understand more English than they let on, so speak slowly and clearly, avoiding idiomatic language and slang.

4. Review What's Been Said — Anticipate What's Coming

After a meeting or during breaks, review with your interpreter the main points made by both sides. Ask what she observed about the other side's position or behavior. Work together to get a feel for the direction in which negotiations are headed, and anticipate what will need to be said later on. Doing this helps your interpreter to prepare the interpretation so that your views will be received in the most favorable possible way.

5. Emphasize Important Points as They Arise

Abstract and complicated discussion is seldom directly translatable; an experienced, qualified interpreter tailors her translations to reflect style, level of formality, tone and intended meaning.

You can help ensure that important points get across by repeating or emphasizing them and by making certain that your verbal and nonverbal messages are consistent with each other. For example, serious concerns should be reflected in your face, the tone of your voice and your bearing.

The Japanese Approach to Contracts

Successful negotiations may result in the signing of a contract, but this is no guarantee that the business relationship is solid. The Japanese consider a contract to be a general commitment to do business, not a document outlining every aspect of a deal. Contracts are seen as far less meaningful than personal commitments between associates. When Japanese do business with each other, they sometimes do so based solely on verbal agreements.

Most contracts in Japan are subject to *jijo henko* ("circumstances change"), which is used to amend or even negate agreements. It's not unusual for there to be a *jijo henko* clause in the initial contract — which means, from a Western point of view, that the contract isn't legally binding!

If a strong relationship has been established and the signatories remain in close cooperation, the contract will usually remain workable. However, if the foreign party is relocated or leaves the company, the Japanese may view the contract as null and void, and insist that it be re-negotiated by new individuals.

Contracts with foreigners are becoming more common in Japan. However, it's important to remember that, while many executives graduated with law degrees, lawyers are uncommon both in Japan and in Japanese companies. It can take months to translate large legal documents into Japanese so that your counterparts can understand them.

 ## Business Outside the Law

The Yakuza

The Yakuza manage a large, pervasive economy dealing in illegal goods and services, particularly real estate. Its attempts to invest its profits in legitimate businesses have led to scandals linking yakuza godfathers with politicians.

The name Yakuza derives from an ancient card game similar to blackjack. The organization brought "socially accepted vices," such as gambling and prostitution, to Japan during the conservative reign of the Tokogawa Shogunate (1603-1867). Today, they rule their fiefdoms with threats, intimidation and violence. They're mostly left untouched by police, as long as there is no overt trouble. Surprisingly, Japanese police often tell victims that they that should not complain because it stirs up trouble.

There are over 2,500 recognized Yakuza gangs in Japan, the largest of which is the Yamaguchi-gumi. Many of the low- and medium-level Yakuza are easy to recognize by their tattoos, white shoes, permed hair, gold teeth, missing knuckles (knuckles are chopped off, one at a time, as punishment for failure) and even little lapel pins that identify their particular affiliation. For the most part, they do not bother foreigners. However, it pays to conduct a background check on your potential business associates; once you're involved with a Yakuza member, it's difficult to sever the relationship.

Besides the Yakuza, there are also the Soukaiya. They extort money in return for leaving citizens alone (thus taking advantage of the Japanese desire for peace and surface harmony). They're a constant fixture at Japanese stockholder meetings, where they verbally abuse the corporate officers and often resort to spitting and even physical assault. Unfortunately, the companies usually encourage them by paying them off.

It should be noted that while street crime hit a postwar high in 1992, it's still negligible when compared with other developed countries.

Graft and Corruption

Traditionally, corrupt politicians were allowed to resign in quiet but affluent disgrace, meanwhile making way for the next candidate from the same party. In the 1970s, a scandal involving payoffs and influence peddling in a major procurement deal with the Lockheed Corporation actually brought down the Takeda government — criminal charges were filed against many top government officials, including then-Prime Minister Takeda. (It's noteworthy that the case against Takeda faced continual and suspicious delays and was not resolved until after his death.) This pattern has since been repeated, most recently in the 1980s by the Recruit scandal, in which a number of political insiders were caught taking illegal stock gifts in return for favors.

Present Changes and Future Outlook

In the early 1990s, a number of major securities firms (with the aid, or at least knowledge, of the government) were found to have reimbursed the investment losses of certain large customers at the expense of smaller investors and the firms' stockholders. The public was outraged.

Voters suddenly became less tolerant in March 1993, when a high-ranking LDP leader was convicted of tax evasion (and, coincidentally, was found to be in possession of US$51 million). Augmented by a lingering recession and a revolt in the party's ranks, the scandal resulted in a stunning upset victory for a newly formed coalition committed to changing the rules for campaign financing and to cleaning up corruption.

The government has made significant inroads toward curbing the Yakuza's influence, and politicians are careful not to appear connected with the organization in any way. But given the degree of overlapping holdings and high-level business cooperation that still exists, insider trading, market manipulation, price fixing and compliance irregularities remain relatively common.

In addition, bid rigging and kickbacks are considered by most observers to be rampant. The importance placed on consensus means that collusive practices tend to be viewed with far more leniency than they would in the West. In fact, some argue that these practices help to even out the distribution of profits, rewards and benefits, thus keeping almost everyone on the inside happy.

Still, the system as a whole can be said to operate in a generally clean (if hardly transparent) fashion, and many of the practices cited by foreign businesses and governments can be attributed to differences in cultural perceptions.

15 Names & Greetings

The Japanese use their surname first, followed by their given name. However, they typically introduce themselves to Westerners using the Western style of given name followed by surname.

Gender and Designations

Until recently, given names often revealed gender by the ending — *ko* (as in *Yukiko, Akiko, Michiko*) or *e* (as in *Yukie, Akie, Michie*) indicated female and *o* (*Kazuo, Yukio, Masao*) or *ro* (*Taro, Ichiro, Kentaro*) indicated male.

But in the past few years, "modern" (and sometimes more Westernized) names have become popular, especially for women (such as Mari or Ami).

The suffix *san* serves as Mr., Mrs. and Miss. For example, Miss Tanaka is referred to as Tanaka-*san*, Mr. Ichikawa as Ichikawa-*san*, etc. *Sensei* (teachers) are addressed as such, so Professor Mori would be Mori-*sensei*. If you want to be particularly respectful, use the honorific *samma* (Yoshida-*samma*), but don't overdo or you might appear to be insincere.

The Japanese will quietly suffer foreigners calling them by their first names, but it's a privilege usually reserved for close family and intimates. When in Europe or the United States, the Japanese may call non-Japanese associates by their first names, but they'll revert back to their traditional style upon returning home.

Bowing

Japan is a very formal culture, and greetings and leave-taking are both important and elaborate. First impressions are likely to set the tone of relationships. If you don't want to drive yourself crazy, accept the fact that you are unlikely to ever master the system. Nonetheless, there are some things you can learn to do.

Bowing is a sign of respect and humility, not subservience. However, if it makes you uncomfortable, a nod of the head will usually serve the same purpose. If you're going to bow, the question is how much and who goes first. The short answer is — you (the guest), and not too deeply. Generally, the person of lower rank goes first and bows lowest. But as a foreigner, you are not expected to follow the rules unless meeting someone of extremely high rank. A proper bow is executed from the waist. For men, hands should be at one's sides; for women, hands rest on one's thighs.

The Importance of Business Cards

Meishi (business cards) are serious tools for establishing business contacts. Failure to present one at a first meeting can indicate that you're unaware of proper business etiquette or that you lack interest.

Always carry an ample supply (at least 100 for a one-week visit), with English on one side and Japanese on the other. If you're not able to have bilingual cards printed in advance of your trip, large hotels in Japan can arrange to have it done for you within twenty-four hours. A Japanese who is familiar with you and your company should verify that the Japanese translation is accurate. Having your name written in Japanese phonetic symbols will prove enormously helpful to your Japanese counterparts.

Protocol dictates that the person of lower rank present his card first. (It doesn't hurt to take the initiative.) Here are some guidelines:

- **Be formal.** Present and receive business cards with both hands and with a certain amount of ceremony. The card should be held between the thumbs and forefingers, with the print facing the recipient.

- **Respect seniority and rank.** Always present your card to the most senior person first.

- **Take your time.** After you receive someone's card, study it carefully for a few seconds, perhaps looking up again at its owner. Then carefully place it on the table or hold it until you sit down.

- **Treat the card with respect.** Business cards are considered to be an extension of the person they represent. You should not write on someone else's business card in his presence; doing so would be comparable to someone writing on your personal property. Don't bend it or drop it, and be sure to not leave it behind.

- **Shaking hands.** A Japanese businessperson will probably not initiate a handshake, but most will readily accept one. Shake hands gently; a Japanese handshake is likely to be as tentative as your bow.

16 Communication Styles

Consider the Context

Japanese communication styles are implicit and nonverbal — that is, highly contextual. The language itself encourages vagueness and ambiguity, which is why *haiku* poetry usually fails to translate well into Western languages. The reader is reduced to a single interpretation of the many possible meanings of the original text.

Traits of Japanese communication include:

- Vagueness and indirection, rather than direct, specific references. Conversations are framed in such a way that they are always open to personal interpretation.

- Sentences are frequently left unfinished, so that the listener can finish them in his own mind.

- A great deal of attention is paid to the tone and levels of politeness (subtleties not easily understood by non-native speakers).

- Listeners frequently repeat "hai" to suggest understanding and encouragement, or to demonstrate that they're following the conversation.

The Mythical Etiquette Book

In virtually all aspects of Japanese culture, from tea ceremonies to baseball games, form is as important, if not more important, than content. Many long-time foreign residents of Japan are convinced that there is a book somewhere (possibly a whole set of books) that outlines every nuance of Japanese behavior for every possible situation. This enormously valuable resource is, however, permanently unavailable to non-Japanese.

Therefore, it's up to you to learn, at first on your own, and later from Japanese friends and personal experiences. The Japanese emphasis on politeness, along with their concern about not causing you to lose face, virtually ensures that they will rarely correct you or give you unsolicited advice in this area.

Guidelines

The following will help you become more conscious of your body language and the ways in which it might be interpreted.

1.   Avoid Physical Contact

The Japanese are uncomfortable with displays of emotion and with physical contact (even a movement as casual to Westerners as loosely touching someone's elbow or shoulder). They certainly do not want to take part in such behavior, and they don't like seeing it displayed by others. Except for shaking hands, it's a good idea not to touch a Japanese.

2.   Keep Your Distance

Westerners typically stand 18 to 24 inches apart; Japanese are most comfortable with a distance of about 36 inches. Standing closer than that will probably force your conversation partner to retreat until he or she is backed up against a wall.

In informal situations (a karaoke bar, for instance), Japanese observe different boundaries, with the distance shrinking noticeably. Westerners may be surprised by the sudden change and be tempted to interpret it as a sign of increasing intimacy. But the next morning, the usual distance will have been reestablished.

All proximity rules are suspended in subways and elevators, where physical contact is unavoidable. Individuals simply withdraw by averting their eyes; thus, they can "touch" without "feeling."

3. Adjust Your Behavior to the Circumstances

Sophisticated travelers are good observers and mimics. Watch your hosts and follow their lead.

4. Speak Softly

Because of the high regard for graciousness and restraint, you should avoid raucous laughter and raising your voice, especially in anger.

5. Keep Your Hands Down

Japanese don't "talk" with their hands, and even if they did, they'd be "speaking" Japanese. So they're not going to understand your gestures. Large hand and arm movements while talking are considered unrefined and rude (at the very least) and possibly threatening. Broad gestures may be interpreted as anger. However, small, effective gestures that illustrate what you're trying to say are much appreciated.

When they're standing, Japanese typically clasp their hands in front of them or keep them at their sides. When seated, they put them on the table in front of them or in their lap.

6. Listen More — Talk Less

Listen carefully, wait for others to finish, and don't talk too much. The most typical complaint that Japanese have about Americans and some Europeans is that they don't do any of the three. Programs that enhance listening skills for Japanese are currently among the most popular corporate training offerings in large Japanese organizations.

7.   Posture Counts

Balance is a much-valued principle that applies to all aspects of Japanese life. Avoid slouching, standing with hands in your pockets or leaning back in a tipped chair; these behaviors will not be well received. Don't lean against the door frame or wall when you're talking with others.

8.   Don't Act Like You Own the Place

Walk slowly and allow your host to be the one obviously in charge. For example, when you're moving around an open area, follow slightly behind him, especially if he is of superior rank. Foreigners, especially those of large stature, should never loom over others — in particular, elders and superiors. It's seen as a sign of disrespect. When passing in front of a Japanese who is seated, it's polite to hunch over a bit, thereby acknowledging his presence.

9.   Don't Point

It's a good idea to avoid pointing altogether (especially at people). To call someone over, extend the hand and fingers, palm down, and "scoop" the air in a downward motion. To get the attention of a waiter, catch his eye and nod your head downward.

These general guidelines will not always be followed by your Japanese hosts, but it's better to err on the side on conservatism. In general, be polite, observant and a bit reserved, and your Japanese hosts will think of you as a *majime* (an unexpectedly pleasing foreigner).

Customs

Shoe Protocol

You'll probably be taking your shoes off at least once during the day, so always wear socks or hosiery that you'll be happy to be seen in. If you see shoes lined up in the entryway to a public or private building, remove yours and align them with the rest. Slippers are generally provided for walking in wooden hallways and should be used. When passing from a wooden hallway to a room with *tatami* (rice mats), leave your slippers in the hall outside the door.

In *ryokan* (traditional Japanese inns) and some restaurants, you will encounter a second pair of slippers, usually red, at the door of the *benjo* (toilet). This tells you that it is empty (or that an uninformed foreigner is using it). Exchange your hallway slippers for the red ones, leaving the former outside the door to alert others, and thus avoid a knock on the door.

Whatever you do, don't return to the inn or dining room in the red slippers, unless you wish to be the focus of great amusement for the other guests.

Ofuro

Bathing and cleanliness are essential aspects of Japanese life, as reflected in the honorific "o" that precedes the word for bath (*furo*). In *ryokan*, hot spring resorts and elsewhere, public baths are still in use. The best ones, old-timers will tell you, are made of cypress wood.

The *ofuro* is a place in which to soak and relax for a few hours, to shed the accumulated tensions of the day and ensure a good night's sleep. Most are separated by sex. For the Japanese, the bath is not a place where sexual thoughts, never mind activities, are appropriate.

Here's the procedure:

- Undress in the locker room area and pick up a towel (usually very small), a piece of soap, and a bucket.

- Your next stop will likely be a large room (with tiled floor and walls) that contains a number of faucets with small stools below them. Sit in front of a faucet, then soap, wash and rinse yourself off. Do this two or three times, making certain to rinse off all the soap.

- The bath will be in an adjoining room and will look more like a swimming pool. (Do not take the soap to the bath! Japanese will not find this even slightly amusing, and they may all leave the *ofuro* until it's drained and refilled.) Protocol is to walk around using the towel in an attempt at modesty, but do not take it into the bath with you. Sometimes it will be used to rinse the face or to absorb perspiration from the head while sitting in the bath.

- The bath water will be very hot. Before getting in, locate one of a number of the cold water faucets that are placed every few feet along the wall above water level. Sit on the edge of the bath and ease yourself in. If it's too hot (and it's almost certainly going to be), turn on the cold water. Try not to overdo this, as you will get increasingly angry looks from the other patrons. Don't stay in too long, and be careful of dizziness when you get out.

- Some baths, especially those in health clubs, have saunas, steam rooms, individual whirlpools, herbal baths, massage tables and lounges in which you can relax, have a cold drink, talk and read. There may also be a complete range of toilet and beauty products available for your use.

Many resorts (used for both company vacations and private visits) have *onsen* (hot springs). Visiting an *onsen* is considered one of the premier experiences in Japan. The same basic rules of the *ofuro* apply, and you may even be served some *atsukan* (hot sake) to make the experience complete.

Gift Giving

Japanese are enthusiastic gift givers. Gifts express friendship and may symbolize hopes for good future business, the conclusion of a successful enterprise, or appreciation for a favor done. The Western habit of simply saying "thank you" for a favor is considered inadequate and possibly insincere. But keep in mind that gifts often have more symbolic than monetary value. Avoid very expensive gifts unless the recipient is a long-time associate who has proved to be particularly important to the success of a venture; they are liable to oblige the recipient to reciprocate with a gift of even greater value.

Although gifts are not expected on a first visit,

you may decide to give them if you feel a relationship has already been started. In an office or business environment, it is best to give gifts such as pens or paperweights with your company's logo. If only one gift is to be given, it should be presented to the head of the Japanese group at a dinner or upon the conclusion of a successful meeting. If gifts are to be given to several individuals, be sure that everyone receives one of approximately equal value or that the most senior executive receives the most valuable gift.

When visiting a Japanese house, bringing a gift of fruit, sweets or items from your native country that aren't readily available in Japan is a good strategy. High-quality Scotch is a particular favorite. T-shirts with slogans in English are popular with children. Avoid giving combs (the Japanese word for comb is *kushi*, *ku* meaning suffering and *shi*, death) or anything in a set of four or nine (*shi* and *ku*, as just mentioned). Flowers are considered a bit ostentatious, but they're acceptable from Westerners. Avoid camellias, lotus blossoms and lilies, all of which are associated with funerals.

Gifts should never be wrapped in black, grey or white paper (funeral colors), and elaborate ribbon bows should be avoided. Japanese do not usually open a gift in front of the giver. However, if you are encouraged to do so, open your gift slowly and carefully. Tearing the paper or opening the gift hastily is considered a sign of greed.

In actuality, the culture of gift giving has snowballed out of hand. Japanese traveling overseas often find gift shopping so time-consuming that there is time for little else. Still, as a general rule, you can never bring too many gifts to Japan, so bring a few extra unassigned ones. At the airport, Japanese custom officers will often wave you by with an understanding look if you mention the word *omiage* (gift) while gesturing at the extra bulging bag you're carrying. Recently, Westerners have coined a new word for this traveling potlatch — *omiagage* — a combination of *omiage* and the English word *baggage* (as in the phrase "excess baggage").

Japanese New Year

The new year is celebrated with an array of symbolic foods — beans for good health, fish roe for prosperity, dried squid for happiness, as well as a midnight New Year's supper of long *soba* noodles (which symbolize carrying the previous year's good fortunes into the new one). Another traditional dish is *ozouni*, a soup that contains a soft rice cake so sticky that the choking deaths of senior citizens are regularly reported in the next day's newspapers. *Toso*, a special mixture of sake and vegetable extracts sweetened with herbs, is also served.

If you're invited to celebrate with a family, it's traditional to bring small amounts of money wrapped in special envelopes for the children.

Beginning at 11 P.M. on New Year's Eve, many Japanese visit *Shinto* (traditional Japanese) shrines. Families spend the next few days either vacationing or staying home to watch TV. The most popular television program is *Kouhaku*, a five-hour showcase competition between the year's most popular singers, judged by a celebrity panel.

18   Dress & Appearance

While Western dress is favored in public, many older Japanese prefer the traditional *kimono* when relaxing at home. (Never fold the right side of the *kimono* over the left; it's symbolic of death.)

The young follow the latest American and European fads. A recent, particularly Japanese trend among teenagers and those in their twenties is *chapatsu* ("tea hair") — dying one's black hair brown. Both sexes, it seems, favor brown-haired dates (more casual and individualistic) but seek out black tresses (more serious) for potential spouses.

Business attire is generally conservative. Dark suits of fine tailoring, and expensive but understated accessories are ideal for both sexes. Men often dress up, even for a golf or fishing trip, but tuxedos are not worn for formal occasions. Because traditional restaurants will have you sitting on the floor, tight skirts and dresses are problematic.

Ryokan (traditional Japanese inns) sometimes supply their guests with *yukata* (light cotton robes), *geta* (wooden clogs), *zori* (sandals) and *tabi* (socks with a split to accommodate *geta* and *zori* thongs).

Reading the Japanese

Style as Substance

Honed through the centuries, social behavior and etiquette are as important in Japanese society as they are intricate. What a person does is often seen as less important than how he or she does it.

Gestures and Expressions

- The meaning of laughter and smiles among Japanese depends upon the situation. When Japanese are nervous or embarrassed, they often smile and laugh nervously. They may be responding to an inconvenient request, a sensitive issue brought up in conversation or to an inadvertent mistake in behavior.

- Japanese cover their mouths for any of a number of reasons, since showing the teeth is taken as a sign of aggression. This applies to yawning, coughing, embarrassment (women especially do this) and using toothpicks in public. (Using toothpicks is not an indication of class in Japan. Everyone does it.)

- The large number of Japanese who wear white gauze masks is always a source of curiosity.

Usually, it's because they have colds and don't wish to pass them along to others.

- Japanese use the "OK" gesture (thumb and forefinger forming a circle) when they want their change from a monetary transaction in coins.

- Japanese point at their nose when indicating themselves.

- Japanese rarely express anger or disappointment, but when they do, it's usually in one or more of the following ways:

  1. A sucking in of breath that produces a "shh" or "sah" sound (often accompanied by head movement to the side).
  2. A blank expression or a sudden unwillingness to make eye contact. (A Japanese may also avoid eye contact so as not to appear aggressive.)
  3. Impatient smiling or nodding.
  4. Repeated glances at a clock or watch.
  5. In a business situation, an inquiry to an assistant or interpreter as to how much longer the meeting will last.
  6. A lingering cold silence in response to a request.

20   Entertaining

Japanese consider their homes private places, and they rarely, if ever, entertain there. It's equally rare for Japanese wives to join their husbands for an evening's entertainment out that's connected with his business. (If she's invited, her husband may well show up without her and offer an excuse.) The general rule for businessmen traveling to Japan is to not bring along their spouses unless expressly invited to do so; the former will be kept so busy into the wee hours by their hosts that wives, sitting at the hotel, will almost always feel neglected. Moreover, inviting your spouse to a business event (entertainment included) will make most Japanese extremely uncomfortable. After you become more at ease with your Japanese associates, there will be opportunities to share more of Japan with your families.

Culinary Wonders

A traditional Japanese breakfast includes rice, seaweed, pickled vegetables and dried fish. For lunch or dinner, you will certainly be offered *sushi* or *sashimi* (raw fish). Both in a desire to offer guests the finest and out of what seems to be a perverse interest in challenging limits, Japanese will sometimes serve visitors very unusual food. Examples include live fish that you must eat while it stares at you, a type of tadpole/lizard that lives in rice fields, and a carefully cleaned — and otherwise poisonous — blowfish called *fugu*. Regional specialties include the wide (and quite palatable) selection of raw horse meat available in Kyushu.

If you're willing to try any or all of these, the Japanese will be delighted; if not, they won't be surprised. In either case, the best tactic is to thank your hosts for giving you such an unusual opportunity.

Geisha Houses

Geisha means "talented person." Though the word connotes prostitution in the West (probably a legacy of drunken U.S. soldiers on leave there), sex hasn't been associated with genuine *geisha* entertainment in modern times. (The first *geisha* date back to 1600, and they were, by the way, men.) Many prostitutes have taken to calling themselves *geisha*, but every Japanese knows the real thing.

By some estimates, there are less than 1000 *geisha* in Japan today. Curators of Japanese tradition, they can sing, play traditional Japanese instruments, dance, and talk entertainingly about almost anything, all in a effort to relax their customers. *Geisha* districts (such as the Gion in Kyoto) are unbelievably expensive ($5,000 an hour per person and up) and increasingly rare.

For true connoisseurs of Japanese culture, geishas are worth any price, but most geisha entertainment is presented in order to demonstrate how well a business can afford to entertain its clients.

Restaurants

Japanese often invite their guests to dinner in a traditional Japanese restaurant. Remove your shoes at the door. The table may be in a reserved private room with rice paper walls and *tatami* (thick floor mats).

The guest of honor (or the highest-ranking associate) is seated farthest away from, and facing, the exit. This custom developed in ancient times — it was the best position from which important samurai could resist attacks by assassins.

Guests are seated on the floor. Men should sit cross-legged, and women should kneel or tuck their legs under them and to one side. Do not resist the urge to stretch. It is not uncommon that, while trying to "be Japanese," foreigners lose all feelings in their legs. Another setup is a *kotatsu* (a table that sits over an opening in the floor). Guests sit with their legs dangling in the opening. In the winter, there might be an electric heater on the bottom of the table. In more remote areas of the country, there might even be a charcoal fire under the table and a quilt to cover diners' legs.

After you sit down, you will be offered an *oshibori* (tightly rolled-up damp cloth). In the winter, the cloth is quite hot, and in the summer, cold. Be careful if you're wearing makeup.

Sake First

Before food is served, everyone drinks a few small cups of *sake*, a potent rice wine, but beer is becoming increasingly common. Tradition calls for the first round to be drunk in unison, after the principal host has spoken a few words of welcome and said the traditional *kan pai* (literally "dry glass," the Japanese equivalent of "bottoms up"). It's proper for the honored guest to return the toast.

Using Chopsticks

Learning to use *hashi* (chopsticks) before you come to Japan will be time well spent. (Silverware is thought to impart an unpleasant taste to food.) After you've learned to hold them correctly, one good way to practice is by picking up peanuts. If you are able to pick up a bowlful with relative ease, you should have no trouble at dinner. Here are a few rules:

- Although it might seem a natural thing to do, it is extremely rude to stick chopsticks upright into a bowl of rice. (It reminds Japanese of the incense burned at funerals.)

- Never use chopsticks to point.

- When taking food from a communal plate, turn your chopsticks around, and pick the food up with the blunt ends to prevent contamination of other people's food. If serving chopsticks are provided, use them.

- Finally, when you are not using your chopsticks, put them down on the chopstick rest provided, not on a bowl or plate.

The Meal Itself

Japanese food, while delicious and pleasing to the eye, is served in portions smaller than those customary in many other countries. Unfortunately for those with large appetites, only second helpings of rice are usually offered, and it's rude to ask for more food.

As a signal to begin eating, your host will pick up his chopsticks and say *itadakimasu*, the Japanese equivalent of the French *bon appetit*. When eating rice, it's proper to pick it up in lumps (it's sticky). Japanese adults usually pick up the rice bowl in order to eat, and they never mix the rice with other food. If you dare to ruin the rice's purity by pouring soy sauce on it, you will certainly get disgusted looks.

If you would like more rice, it's customary to leave a few grains in your bowl and put down your chopsticks. Finishing all your rice is a signal that you've finished eating.

Conversation, Cigarettes and the Check

Many Japanese do not engage in conversation during a meal. Westerners, who sometimes find silence uncomfortable, should resist the temptation to keep talking just to avoid silence.

Cigarettes are often smoked throughout the meal. It's perfectly acceptable to decline, but it's considered quite rude to ask the host and other guests to refrain. Smoking is currently on a slight decline among Japanese men, but on a big upswing among Japanese women.

At the end of the meal, you will probably not see the check. If one comes, your Japanese host will pay it; offering to split the bill is considered rude. Tipping is not customary. Accepting an invitation to dinner puts you in debt to your host; repay the favor by inviting him out later for a meal.

Dining Out Alone

The most common problem non-Japanese have in Japan is finding a place to eat. The variety of restaurants in big Japanese cities is staggering, with some of the best ones hidden in a maze of basements and high-rise towers. Japanese usually only go to restaurants that they know, and many foreigners give up and go to the hotel or to McDonalds.

Asking Japanese friends can help, but many times it can create an obligation to take you there. If you can't read Japanese, ask your hotel about popular dining districts and walk around. Many restaurants have amazingly realistic *shokuhin sampuru* (food samples) displayed in the window. These plastic replicas range from humble bowls of *soba* (buckwheat) noodles to minutely detailed lobsters. Just point something out to the waiter.

The larger cities offer everything from Italian to Indian to Thai cuisine, but many of these have been Japanicized. The Chinese food varies greatly from what you'll find in Chinese countries; pizza can be topped with corn, squid or seaweed, and hot dog buns may have fried noodles inside.

Some of the more common Japanese foods you may taste are:

Tempura — lightly battered seafood and vegetables

Udon — thick soft noodles, served hot or cold

Oden — a variety of fishcakes, vegetables and eggs served in fish broth

Shabu-shabu — meat, shrimp and vegetables that you cook at your table in boiling water

Yakitori — chicken and vegetables grilled on bamboo skewers

Kushiage/kushiyaki — a variety of items on wooden skewers, served one at a time, until you stay "stop"

Kaiseki — traditional Japanese meal consisting of many small, delicately arranged dishes

~don — food served over a bowl of rice

Kobe beef is arguably the best tasting (and definitely the most expensive) beef in the world. Wagu cows are feed an exclusive beer diet, and their stomachs are massaged regularly to ensure perfect marbling of the meat. (Wagus are jealously protected to keep the Japanese monopoly on them. Recently, there was a highly publicized incident in which allegedly stolen wagu sperm was auctioned off, for an unspecified price, in the U.S.)

After Dinner, What?

Finding postprandial entertainment can be as difficult as finding a restaurant. Some clubs are patronized by only one company or group; others charge astronomical prices (and prices are almost never written down). Fortunately, many clubs will politely refuse you entry if they see a tentative look on your face.

Izakaiya (drinking places) are a great place to meet Japanese. There are also "shot bars," which are somewhat similar to Western drinking holes. In Tokyo, there are three major entertainment districts — Shinjuku, Shibuya and Roppongi. All are relatively English friendly, and some stay open as late as 5 A.M.

Roppongi, in particular, deserves some attention. Known as "the foreigner's section" of town, it's really the only international district in Japan. Here, Japanese can mingle with Americans, Australians, Europeans, Asians, Indians, you name it, at numerous clubs and bars. It is a great place to swap stories and information, and if you want, you can usually order a hamburger.

Getting Around

Taxis are everywhere in major cities, but they're expensive. Fortunately, Japan has a very highly developed public transportation system. In most cities, station names appear in roman characters, but it's a good idea to carry a bilingual transportation map, just in case — along with the name

card of your hotel. And keep in mind that the last
trains from Tokyo depart around midnight. If you
miss the last train, you may get into a taxi bidding
war.

Many Japanese who miss the last train decide
to stay downtown and go straight to work in the
morning. If you choose this alternative, there is a
place designed just for such occasions — *capuseru
hoteru* (the capsule hotel). These resemble stacked
coffins. They're inexpensive and, except for the capsule love hotels (don't ask), they have room for
only one (horizontal) person. Still, tiny as their hon-
eycomb compartments are, each contains a bed,
miniaturized air conditioner, clock radio, night-
light, color TV and video.

Unfortunately, most reputable hotels don't take
late guests. But if all else fails, there are all-night
"blue" movie theaters full of snoring businessmen.

21 Socializing

Businessmen typically work long hours, then fraternize until very late. Important decisions and critical problem solving often take place in restaurants and bars, where the rules of engagement are more relaxed. Foreign men are liable to be asked why they have beards, or about the dating behavior of women in their country. Foreign women might experience flirtatious or demeaning behavior that makes them uncomfortable, but it is rarely unmanageable.

The Japanese Pub Crawl

The Japanese are among the heaviest drinkers in Asia, a trait that has been attributed to the society's tendency to stifle the individual. Many Japanese find license in alcohol and become unusually boisterous and assertive only when they are drunk (or even have a drink in their hand).

If you stay in Japan long enough, you will inevitably be invited for an evening of *hashigo* (literally "ladder drinking"). Take it as a sign that you are being accepted as a peer; refusing to go may be interpreted as aloofness.

Typically, the party will begin at an elegant, expensive spot, then move down the class and economic scales as the evening progresses. Beer is served in large bottles that are shared by all, and drunk from small glasses. You should not pour a drink for yourself, but allow others to do it. Likewise, you should pour drinks for others whenever you get the chance. Never ask someone to pour a drink for you; wait for them to offer.

Karaoke: Star in Your Own Music Video

Karaoke literally means "empty orchestra." In karaoke clubs, groups of (often inebriated) friends and associates take turns singing pop songs to each other. Most clubs feature a raised platform with a standing microphone, above which is a television monitor that displays videos depicting the song's story, with the lyrics at the bottom of the screen.

According to one estimate, a karaoke microphone is warbled into in Japan about 16.5 million times a day. The phenomenon has burgeoned into a $10 billion industry. One video game company is now sending karaoke music into Japanese homes, on demand, through telephone lines. The Asaka Beer Corporation has come up with a hydrogen-laced brew said to help singers reach the high notes.

Expect to be called upon to sing at least once. Ignorance of Japanese music will not save you, and any attempt, no matter how poor, will be greeted with much praise and applause. (Popular English-language songs include *My Way, Yesterday, I Left My Heart in San Francisco, Country Roads* and *The Girl from Ipanema*.) Higher-class clubs have private rooms in which patrons can sing and drink until the sun comes up; some have "hostesses" who pour drinks, make small talk, sing duets and dance with you.

Karaoke singing is one of the very few socially

acceptable ways in which an individual can display his or her talent without being branded arrogant or self-centered. It fulfills the latent desire to gain credit as an individual without jeopardizing the need to be accepted by the whole group and is an excellent way to establish close relations with the Japanese.

Golf

Golf, a relatively new Western import, is a high-status game throughout Asia, and the Japanese are *gorufu kichigai* ("nuts about golf"). Japanese variations on the game include using old ladies as caddies, taking long breaks for lunch, and soaking in an *ofuro* after the round.

Because most golf courses are in outlying areas, the Japanese send their clubs ahead via *takyubin* (delivery service). This method has become so popular, that at many golf courses, a delivery service representative keeps a permanent desk at the clubhouse. Golfing with a Japanese associate has the advantage of being an activity that can be shared without the need for strong verbal communication.

Membership in golf courses is prohibitively expensive, but urban driving ranges, open both day and night, are popping up all over the country; due to lack of space, some nestle atop downtown buildings. Or try a golf "simulator." Your favorite course is projected onto a large canvas; after you hit your ball into the imaginary scene, your shot is tracked, and its trajectory monitored, by video.

Sumo

Probably the most traditional of Japanese sports, sumo spectacles were originally an aspect of rice planting and harvest seasons. Today, considerable ritual both precedes and follows a match, in which enormous men dressed in silk loincloths grapple each other (rounds usually last less than one minute) until the loser is hurled from the ring or knocked down.

Sumo wrestlers live in *heya* (stables), where they train and eat enormous amounts of fish, vegetables, tofu, seaweed, eggs and rice, washed down with beer. After gorging themselves, they sleep, with the food turning happily to fat. One of the few American sumo, Konishiki (Salevaa Atisnoe by his Hawaiian name), was the heaviest sumo of all time, weighing in at 219.5 kg (484 lbs.). Another Hawaiian American, Akebono (Chad Rowhan), a.k.a. "The Dawn," became the first foreign *yokuzuna* (grand champion).

Sumo wrestlers wear their hair in 18th century topknots slicked down with aromatic grease; when they retire, their topknots are cut off in the presence of their professional elders. They're considered sex symbols, and pictures of them with their tiny, glamourous model girlfriends appear in newspapers throughout the country. Unfortunately, professional tournaments are held only six times a year, and tickets, if available, are extraordinarily expensive. The good news is that with its short rounds, sumo is ideal for broadcasting on TV and for instant replays.

Pachinko

Japan's leading indoor sport is a vertical pinball game, usually played in gaudy arcades. Pachinko addicts include everyone from teenagers to grandmothers, from housewives to businessmen. Winners receive prizes (candy, toothpaste, socks), which can be exchanged for cash in nearby blackmarket buy-back booths.

Originally, miniature steel balls were shot up one at a time, but today, variations include machine-gun-like, rapid-fire play, Las Vegas-style "one-arm bandits," and even machines with built-in televisions. The Institute of Pachinko Technology is only one of many schools offering instruction in the finer points of the game for serious players.

If you want to try, expect clanking balls accompanied by blaring music, blinding fluorescent lights, billowing clouds of cigarette smoke, and occasional stares from amused Japanese.

Japanese Theatre: Noh and Kabuki

The slow, mesmerizing world of the noh play was a favorite of medieval Japanese military nobility. The masks, chanting, sparse settings and spare musical accompaniment (flute and drums) are hypnotic. The plays usually revolve around two characters, one a trapped spirit, the other a wandering priest. On summer nights, they're sometimes performed under the stars, illuminated by torchlight.

Traced back to a provocative, frolicking dance of a woman named Okuni, kabuki (literally, "song dance skill") became the cultural choice of 16th century mercantile Japan. When the overtly sexual themes of early kabuki were rooted out by a conservative government, female actors were replaced by *onnagata* (female impersonators). By the 20th century, *onnagata* had become the most famous of all kabuki actors, and kabuki soon evolved into an all-male form.

Unlike noh, kabuki features sumptuous costumes (which force the actors to make spectacular gestures), brilliant makeup (crimson = justice, blue = evil), and beautifully designed stages filled with such gimmicks as trap doors. Performances last all day, and it's not unusual for the audience to go out and grab a snack while the play's in progress.

22   Basic Japanese Phrases

English	Japanese
Yes No	*Hai* *Iie*
Good morning Hello (daytime) Hello (evening) Hello (telephone)	*Ohayo-gozaimasu* *Konichiwa* *Konbanwa* *Moshi-moshi*
Good-bye	*Sayonara*
Please	*Dozo*
Thank you	*Arigato*
Pleased to meet you	*Hajimemashite*
Excuse me; I'm sorry	*Sumimasen*
My name is _____	*Watashi wa _____ desu*
I don't understand	*Wakarimasen*
Do you speak English?	*Eigo o hanashimasu ka?*
Can we meet tomorrow?	*Ashita oai deki masu ka?*

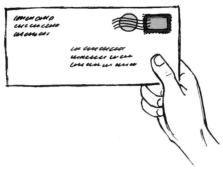

Correspondence

In general, the order of information in a Japanese mailing address (written in Roman letters) is the same as in most Western countries. For example:

Mr. Ken Murakami, Vice President
Kansai Telecom Co., Ltd.
1111 3-chome, Yamato-dori
Kita-ku,
Osaka 557

It's useful to recognize the following words in addresses: Kita (North), Minami (South), Higashi (East), Nishi (West) and Chua (Central).

Japanese dates are abbreviated. For example, H.8.2.29, meaning February 29, 1996 in the 8th year of the Heisei era of reign. For international business purposes, Japanese would write the date 96.2.29 or 29.2.96.

24 Useful Numbers

These are local numbers in Japan. If dialing from outside Japan, you must use your country's international access code and the Japan country code [81]. When calling long distance from within Japan, dial "0" before the city code.

- International operator 0051
- Fire/Ambulance 119
- Police 110
- Tokyo police, English-speaking .... (3) 3501-0110
- Japan Helpline, emergency, toll-free
  .... (0120) 461-997
- Japan Airlines .... (3) 3456-2111
  Tourist Information Tokyo.............. (3) 3503-4400
- Japan Travel, toll-free
  .... Eastern Japan (0120) 222-800
  .... Western Japan (0120) 444-800
- Japan Railways, English-speaking
  .... (3) 3423-0111
- FedEx Tokyo .... (3) 3521-4300
- FedEx, toll-free in Japan .... (0120) 003200
- Avis Car Rental .... (3) 3496-0919
- Hertz Car Rental .... (3) 3349-3631

Books & Internet Addresses

The Japanese Mind: The Goliath Explained, by Robert C. Christopher. Linden Press: Simon & Schuster, New York, USA, 1983. One of the best books about contemporary Japanese society. The author is an experienced journalist with an in-depth knowledge of Japan.

Japanese Etiquette and Ethics in Business, by Boye DeMenthe. NTC Business Books, Lincoln-wood, Illinois, USA, 1991. Explains the habits and beliefs that have come to epitomize the Japanese character and business personality.

Culture Shock! Japan, by Rex Shelly. Graphic Arts Center Publishing Company, Portland, Oregon, USA, 1993. A humorous introduction to many of the seemingly incomprehensible facets of Japanese culture. Provides foreigners preparing for a lengthy stay in Japan with helpful tips.

Learning to Bow, by Bruce Feeler. Houghton-Mifflin Company, New York, USA, 1992. Examines bowing as a metaphor for Japan's unique culture.

Japanese Business Etiquette, by Diana Rowland. Warner Books, New York, USA, 1988. A short, easy-to-read explanation of key etiquette elements, from a woman's point of view.

Internet Addresses

World Wide Web Servers in Japan
http://www.ntt.jp/SQUARE/www-in-JP.html

Yahoo! Japan
http://www.yahoo.com/docs/info/
bridge.html

Cyberspace Japan
http://www.csj.co.jp/index.html

Japan Telephone Directory (for Tokyo, Osaka and Kyoto, in English)
http://www.pearnet.org/jtd/

JIN: Japan Information Network (Japan Center for Intercultural Communications)
http://jin.jcic.or.jp/

Usenet Groups
clari.world.asia.japan

World Trade Press
Passport to the World Series
Your Pocket Guide to Business, Culture and Etiquette

These pragmatic, engaging paperbacks contain detailed information about a country's business practices, negotiating style, etiquette, government, work environment, social mores, view of foreigners and much more.

Discover a wealth of hard-to-find information to help you break through cultural barriers and ease any fears about doing business in countries around the globe.

Passport Books are attractively illustrated, easy to read, portable and short enough to digest in one sitting.

Other Passport to the World Books

• Passport ARGENTINA • Passport BRAZIL
• Passport CHINA • Passport FRANCE
• Passport GERMANY • Passport HONG KONG
Passport INDIA • Passport INDONESIA
• Passport ISRAEL • Passport ITALY • Passport KOREA
• Passport MEXICO • Passport PHILIPPINES
• Passport POLAND • Passport RUSSIA
• Passport SINGAPORE • Passport SOUTH AFRICA
• Passport SPAIN • Passport TAIWAN
• Passport THAILAND • Passport UNITED KINGDOM
• Passport USA • Passport VIETNAM
Available from your local bookseller or order direct.

 WORLD TRADE PRESS®
Professional Books for International Trade
1450 Grant Avenue, Suite 204
Novato, California 94945 USA
Tel: (415) 898-1124, Fax: (415) 898-1080
e–mail: WorldPress@aol.com
USA Order Line: (800) 833-8586